Electricity

MATT MULLINS

Children's Press®
An Imprint of Scholastic Inc.
New York Toronto London Auckland Sydney
Mexico City New Delhi Hong Kong
Danbury, Connecticut

Content Consultant
Suzanne E. Willis, PhD
Professor and Assistant Chair, Department of Physics
Northern Illinois University
DeKalb, Illinois

Library of Congress Cataloging-in-Publication Data

Mullins, Matt.
  Electricity/Matt Mullins.
     p. cm.—(A true book)
  Includes bibliographical references and index.
  ISBN-13: 978-0-531-26319-8 (lib. bdg.)   ISBN-10: 0-531-26319-3 (lib. bdg.)
  ISBN-13: 978-0-531-26581-9 (pbk.)   ISBN-10: 0-531-26581-1 (pbk.)
  1. Electricity—Juvenile literature. I. Title.
  QC527.2.M85 2012
  537—dc23   2011016235

All rights reserved. Published in 2012 by Children's Press, an imprint of Scholastic Inc.
Printed in China 62
SCHOLASTIC, CHILDREN'S PRESS, A TRUE BOOK, and associated logos are trademarks and/or registered trademarks of Scholastic Inc.
1 2 3 4 5 6 7 8 9 10 R 21 20 19 18 17 16 15 14 13 12

Find the Truth!

Everything you are about to read is true *except* for one of the sentences on this page.

Which one is **TRUE**?

T or F   Electricity can be found in nature.

T or F   Electricity travels well through wood.

Find the answers in this book.

Contents

THE **BIG** TRUTH!

Amazing Electricity Farms

Magnet with paper clip chain

Insulated copper wire

4 From Batteries to Motors

5 Electricity Comes Home

Flashlights were first called electric lamps or lanterns.

We use electricity every day.

CHAPTER 1

Life Is Electric!

Did you turn on a reading light before opening this book? That is one way to start learning about electricity. Electricity is everywhere. We use it for light, for heat, and for sound. We cook with it. It powers our computers. It keeps our food cold in the refrigerator or freezer. If you use an iPod or MP3 player, you use electricity. Do you watch TV or talk on a phone? If you do, you use electricity!

The first electric light was created in 1808.

Positive and Negative

Electricity is a kind of energy that flows through material. It starts in the atoms that make up everything around us. The structure of atoms helps make electricity. Atoms have tiny particles called **protons** in their centers. Protons have positive charges. Tiny particles called **electrons** circle around the edges of atoms. Electrons have negative charges.

Most modern kitchens are filled with electrical devices.

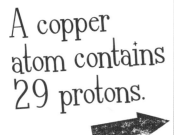

A copper atom contains 29 protons.

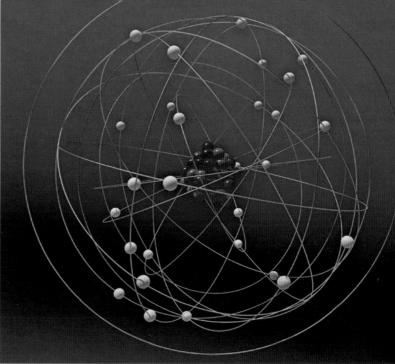

Scientists use colored spheres and circles to create diagrams of atoms.

Opposites Attract

The key to electricity is that opposite charges attract. Electrons and protons are attracted to each other. They are like the opposite ends of magnets. When close, they pull together. When an electron moves away from one atom, it searches for a positive charge on another atom to connect to. When electrons move from atom to atom, they can be directed into streams we call electricity.

Electricity travels to your home along power lines.

From Power Plant to Home

Electrons travel easily through certain materials, like some metals. We can guide electricity through these materials. Electrons can travel for hundreds of miles through big power cables from power plants to homes far away. When you flip on a light switch, streams of electrons pass through the base of the lightbulb. Your light comes on because these electrons power the bulb.

Shocking!

Electrons are in everything, because atoms are in everything. So electricity doesn't just run in wires and cables we make. It occurs in nature as **static electricity**. Static electricity causes you to get a little shock sometimes after walking on a rug. It also causes lightning. We live in a great big field of electricity. Life would be impossible without it!

Lightning is one form of naturally occurring electricity.

Joseph Thomson announced his discovery of the electron in 1897.

Flashlights allow us to see in the dark.

CHAPTER 2

Circuits

Electricity powers things at your home in a simple loop. A wire carries electricity from a power source to the thing being powered, then back to the source. This loop is called a **circuit**. Think about a flashlight. A flashlight uses a circuit. It uses metal wires and batteries to create a loop. Wires go from the batteries to the bulb and back to the batteries to complete the circuit.

The first flashlight was created in 1898.

Some devices, such as this super-bright flashlight, require very powerful batteries.

Switching On, Switching Off

The key to a flashlight circuit is the switch. It separates the wires when it is in the off position. When it is on, it pushes two ends of the wire together. The circuit is closed when the switch is on. Then electrons can flow through the circuit. They pass through the wires and through the batteries. They follow the circuit and run through the base of the bulb. The light goes on.

If you turn the switch off, you disconnect the wires. The circuit is opened, and the bulb goes off. The lights and power in your home operate the same way. The electrical circuit is open until you turn a light switch on. At power outlets, the openings are where a circuit is open. Pushing in the metal prongs of a plug closes the circuit. Electricity runs into your power cord.

Thomas Edison made many important discoveries about electricity.

In 1880, Thomas Edison invented a lightbulb that could last 1,200 hours.

Insulators

Power cords are often coated with plastic or vinyl. The atoms in plastic and vinyl have electrons that stick well to their atoms. Wood, glass, **ceramic**, and fabric have similarly sticky atoms. They all make good **insulators**. Electricity does not move well through them. Insulators are used to cover flashlights, wires, and power outlets. Because of insulators, you can touch these things without getting shocked.

Electricians use insulators to protect them at work.

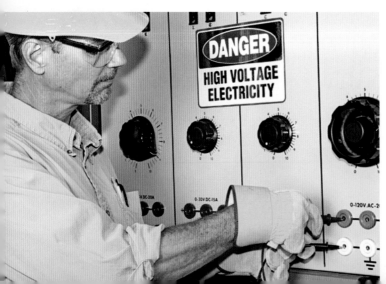

Cotton, silk, and other natural fibers often used in clothes are great insulators.

Metal wires are wrapped in insulating plastic.

Most electrical wiring in houses is made of copper.

Conductors

Most metals have restless electrons. The electrons move away from their atoms pretty easily. Loose electrons flow well through metals. We call materials such as metals **conductors**. They conduct, or move, electricity well. That's why we use metal wires in electric cords and cables. It's why flashlights have metal springs that hold batteries in place. Electricity easily moves through metal wires and metal springs.

Water Can Be Shocking!

The small amounts of minerals and other materials in most water make it an excellent conductor. Electrical shocks can be extremely dangerous, so you need to be careful around water. After you wash your hands, make sure your hands are dry before you touch an electric plug or switch. Don't keep radios and hair dryers near the sink, bath, or shower. When you clean or swim, you want to keep any electrical current out of the water!

Direct Current

Batteries, like magnets, have a positive end and a negative end. A flashlight won't work if its batteries are not lined up properly. What happens if the positive ends of the batteries are pointing toward each other? The electrons will bump into one another and stop. We line batteries up so that the positive end of one battery is touching the negative end of the other. Then electricity can run in a **direct current** (DC).

A flashlight's batteries must be lined up just right for it to work.

You can also try rubbing a balloon on your head to see static electricity at work.

CHAPTER 3

Nature Is Static

You can create static electricity. If you rub a balloon on your sweater, the balloon will gather electrons. The electrons move from your sweater to the balloon. They give the balloon a negative charge. The sweater is left with a built-up positive charge. Place the balloon against the sweater. The opposite charges attract each other. The balloon stays on the sweater even when you take your hand away!

Electricity in your body makes your heart muscle contract and pump blood through your body.

Sparks Fly

The same kind of electron exchange happens when you walk around on a carpet. Your feet rub on the carpet and collect electrons. The electrons cling to you and wait for a chance to move. You reach for a doorknob, and a tiny spark crackles. The electrons have found a positive match and an easy path. Your body acts as a conductor. The electrons jump to the doorknob, and you get a small shock!

Cloudy With a Chance of Electricity

Clouds carry small particles of ice. When wind blows around inside the clouds, it rubs against the ice. This loosens electrons. The top of the cloud loses electrons and builds up a positive charge. The bottom of the cloud loads up with negative charges. For a while, it stays this way. Air separates the charges, and air is a very good insulator.

Franklin wrote a book titled *Experiments and Observations on Electricity*. ➡️

In 1752, Benjamin Franklin used a kite with a metal key attached to prove that lightning was electric.

Lightning bolts are one of nature's amazing sights.

On average, lightning strikes somewhere in the world between 50 and 100 times per second.

Lightning!

Sometimes the separated charges build up enough so that air can no longer insulate them. A stream of electricity flows in the clouds. Then we see **sheet lightning** flashing inside the cloud.

Sometimes negative charges at the bottom of the storm clouds build up. They become strong enough to push away negative charges on the ground. Then the ground has a strong positive charge. Soon electrons jump from the sky to the ground. You see a lightning bolt!

Nature's Batteries

Electric eels are found in South America. They have thousands of special, layered cells in their bodies. Chemicals, like those in a battery, race through these cells when the eel feels threatened. The cells discharge all at once. Then a burst of electricity shocks predators. The shock is five times the strength of the electricity in a wall socket! The eels use smaller charges to kill or stun fish for food.

Electric eels can grow to be 9 feet (2.75 meters) long.

Certain ocean rays and an African catfish also discharge electricity.

Amazing Electricity Farms

One way to make electricity is by using wind. Huge blades, like those on a fan, are attached to tall, metal towers. The wind turns the fans. Moving parts attached to the fan blades create electricity. These towers are put up in fields and on hills that get a lot of wind. Have you ever seen one of these areas? You probably saw dozens, maybe even hundreds, of tall wind towers. We call these places wind farms!

The largest wind farm in the world is in Roscoe, Texas. It has 627 towers.

The world's largest offshore wind farm is the Thanet Wind Farm. It is located 7 miles (11 kilometers) off the coast of England.

Solar farms use thousands of solar panels to take in the sun's energy. The panels then turn this energy into electricity that can be distributed to homes and businesses.

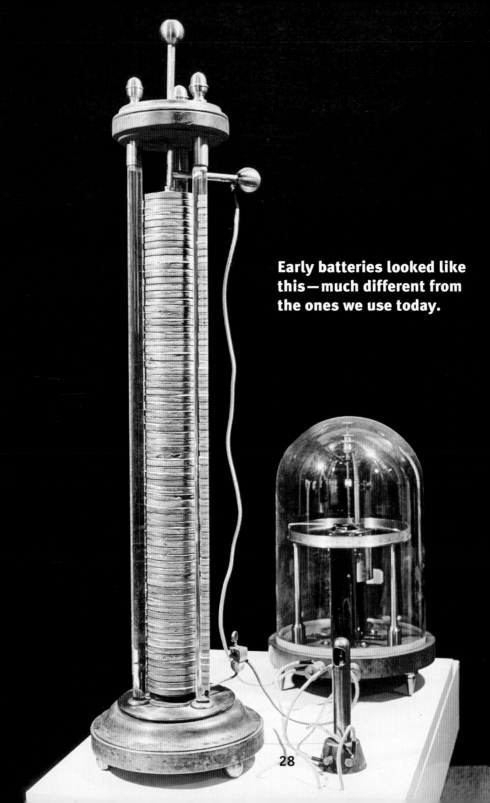

Early batteries looked like this—much different from the ones we use today.

CHAPTER 4

From Batteries to Motors

In 1936, a puzzling clay pot was found in a village near Baghdad, Iraq. It was almost 2,000 years old. In it stood an iron rod wrapped in copper. The rod stuck out from the copper above the lip of the pot. The rod was sealed to the pot with pitch, a sticky substance made from tar. Scientists believe it was a battery. It was probably used for electricity!

Scientists continue to create stronger and longer-lasting batteries.

Volta's Battery

In 1800, Alessandro Volta stacked plates of zinc with plates of silver. He separated them with paper soaked in salt water. He attached these plates to flat copper wires. Volta's device sent electricity through the wires. He became famous for creating the first battery. That is because we didn't know about the battery in Iraq. The Baghdad Battery was probably made about 1,600 years before Volta's battery!

Electricity is measured in volts, a unit named after Alessandro Volta.

Until Volta's battery, scientists only knew about static electricity. Static electricity produces a shock and then disappears. Volta's battery created a stream or **current** of electricity. It didn't go away just as soon as it appeared. Scientists began wondering if we could use this steady power supply. Years later, Englishman Michael Faraday figured out a new use for electricity— moving things!

Michael Faraday built upon Volta's ideas.

Faraday, Magnets, and Electricity

Faraday noticed that magnets and electricity work in similar ways. A magnet has a north and a south pole, similar to a battery's positive and negative ends. When a magnet is close to a paper clip, it turns the paper clip into another magnet. The paper clip's poles line up with the magnet's. Each north pole is attracted to the other's south pole. If the paper clip could move through the magnet, it would be pulled in one end and pushed out the other.

Magnets are named after Magnesia, an area in Greece.

Inventor Michael Faraday's electric motor led to many of the devices we use today.

Like electricity, the force in magnets seems to move in one direction. Imagine linking many paper clips together into a wheel. Then place a magnet in the center space of this wiry circle. What happens to the wheel if you spin the magnet? The wheel spins! Spin the wheel and what happens to the magnet? The magnet spins! Inside the metal, the electrons are attracted to the magnet. They move with the magnet.

Faraday's Electric Motor

Now hold the metal wheel still, and spin the magnet. What happens to the electrons inside the wheel? They rush through the wheel. Electrons that move through metal are electricity! If the metal or the magnet is still, the electrons move. In 1831, Faraday put a magnet inside a coil of copper wires. The magnet moved the coil and created electricity, demonstrating **electromagnetic force**. Faraday used electricity to move metal. He created the first electric motor!

Timeline of Electricity

1800
Alessandro Volta creates a chemical battery.

1831
Michael Faraday builds the first electric motor.

1880
Thomas Edison introduces the first practical incandescent lightbulb.

How Does a Motor Work?

Motors work similarly today. A coil of wire is placed between magnets. A power source, such as a battery, provides electricity to power the magnet. On one side, the magnet pulls at the coil. On the other side, the magnet pushes it. The coil spins, turning electricity into motion. This spins a rod that is attached to the coil. The rod can move things, like blades on a fan. The electricity can send power to things, such as wheels on a toy car.

1893
Tesla demonstrates an alternating current power system and sells it to a power company.

1895
A power company finishes a 22-mile (35.4 km) power line that brings electricity to Sacramento, California.

1891
Nikola Tesla transforms low-voltage electricity to high-voltage in his Tesla coil.

Motors and Power Plants

Power plants are the opposite of motors. They turn motion into electricity. Water is heated into steam. Steam pushes through tubes to a big **turbine,** a rod with wheels or blades like those on a fan. The turbine connects to a big magnet inside a room lined with metal coils. The steam hits the turbine blades with force like wind. The turbine and magnet spin. The magnet generates electricity in the coils. Cables carry the electricity to homes and other buildings.

Power plants use turbines like these to produce vast amounts of electricity.

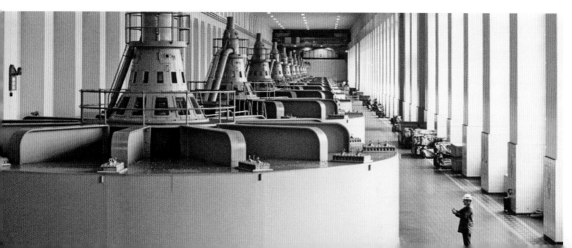

The electric hand drill was invented in 1895.

Life With Motors

Modern life would be difficult to imagine without electric motors. They are used in fans and heaters. They power refrigerators and dryers. They drive power drills.

Drills and other power tools have made work easier for carpenters.

They pull passenger trains. Before Faraday's electric motor, people used steam engines for power. These were huge and difficult to manage. Faraday's invention changed the world! It brought machinery into everyday life.

Substations convert electricity to the right voltage for homes and businesses.

CHAPTER 5

Electricity Comes Home

Before electricity could be sent to homes, scientists had to solve a problem. Metal is not perfectly smooth. It has tiny flaws inside it. As electrons move through metal in one direction, they bump into these flaws. They bounce against each other. This bouncing creates heat. It also sends electrons away. Cables were losing too much electricity! Scientists had to figure out how to stop too many electrons from bouncing away.

The first power plant began operating in 1882 in New York City.

In the late 1800s, inventor and engineer Nikola Tesla discovered a way to take low-voltage electricity and transform it into high-voltage electricity. Soon after, he solved the problem of moving electrons by using an **alternating current** (AC). The alternating current sends electrons in one direction for a brief time, then in another. This helps electrons avoid bouncing around too much. Alternating currents lose less electricity in power lines than direct currents do.

Tesla worked in a laboratory in Colorado Springs for several months in 1899 and 1900.

Tesla was close friends with the writer Mark Twain.

Cities Use Multiple Circuits

Some Christmas tree lights line up in single circuits. Electricity runs through the lights one by one. If one light goes out, it interrupts the flow of electrons. Then all the lights go out. Cities are wired differently. Power is directed from the main circuit onto many branches of lines that loop back to the main line. When a bulb on one of these loops goes out, it does not affect the others.

Edison and Tesla argued about whether DC or AC was better for power systems.

Electricity is used in almost all aspects of modern life.

Tesla's alternating current system allows power companies to send electricity over many miles in high-voltage currents. At the ends of these lines, the electricity can be transformed into low-voltage electricity. This less powerful electricity can be sent short distances to buildings, streetlamps, and homes. Power lines can carry electrons hundreds of miles to your bedroom. Then you can turn on your reading light! ★

True Statistics

Speed of lightning bolts: Up to 130,000 mph (209,215 kph)

Heat of a lightning bolt: Almost 54,000 °F (30,000 °C)

Voltage emitted by an electric eel: Up to 600 volts

Voltage from a typical flashlight battery: 1.5 volts

Potential voltage from a lightning bolt: 3 million volts

Number of homes powered by a typical power plant: 188,000

Number of miles of electric power transmission lines in the United States: More than 186,400 mi. (300,000 km)

Did you find the truth?

(T) Electricity can be found in nature.

(F) Electricity travels well through wood.

Resources

Books

Boothroyd, Jennifer. *All Charged Up: A Look at Electricity*. Minneapolis: Lerner Publications, 2011.

Knapp, Brian. *Simple Electricity*. Vol. 12 of *Science Matters!* New York: Grolier Educational, 2003.

Knapp, Brian. *Changing Circuits*. Vol. 25 of *Science Matters!* New York: Grolier Educational, 2003.

Lockwood, Sophie. *Super Cool Science Experiments: Electricity*. Ann Arbor, MI: Cherry Lake Publishing, 2010.

Masters, Nancy Robinson. *How Did That Get to My House? Electricity*. Ann Arbor, MI: Cherry Lake Publishing, 2010.

Pryor, Kimberley Jane. *Venom, Poison, and Electricity*. New York: Marshall Cavendish Benchmark, 2010.

Whiting, Jim. *The Science of Lighting a City: Electricity in Action*. Mankato, MN: Capstone Press, 2010.

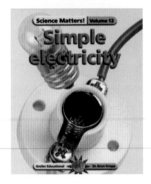

Organizations and Web Sites

Physics4Kids.Com—Electricity and Magnetism

www.physics4kids.com/files/elec_intro.html

Learn about electricity, electrons, charges, currents, and more.

Scholastic—Electricity Online

www2.scholastic.com/browse/article.jsp?id=2847

Learn about electricity, its history, and more.

Places to Visit

American Museum of Radio and Electricity

1312 Bay Street
Bellingham, WA 98225
(360) 738-3886
http://amre.us

Visit exhibits and enjoy kid-friendly programs about electricity and radio and their history.

The Bakken Museum

3537 Zenith Avenue South
Minneapolis, MN 55416-4623
(612) 926-3878
www.thebakken.org

Visit exhibits and take workshops on electricity, inventing, and more.

Important Words

alternating current (ALL-tuhr-nayt-ing KUR-uhnt)—flow of electricity in changing directions

ceramic (suh-RAM-ik)—objects made from clay

circuit (SIR-kit)—a complete path for an electrical current

conductors (kun-DUK-tuhrz)—materials through which electricity can travel

current (KUR-uhnt)—the flow of electricity in a circuit

direct current (dih-REKT KUR-uhnt)—flow of electricity in one direction

electromagnetic force (i-LEK-troh-mag-NET-ik FORS)—the force that moves electric charges

electrons (i-LEK-trahnz)—tiny, negatively charged particles that move around the nucleus of an atom

insulators (IN-sul-lay-turz)—materials that are able to stop heat, electricity, or sound from escaping

protons (PROH-tahnz)—positively charged particles inside the nucleus of an atom

sheet lightning (SHEET LITE-neeng)—lightning that spreads out within a cloud

static electricity (STAT-ik i-lek-TRIS-i-tee)—electricity that builds up in an object as a result of friction

turbine (TUR-bine)—an engine turned by a fluid or steam

Index

Page numbers in **bold** indicate illustrations

About the Author

Matt Mullins holds a master's degree in the history of science from the University of Wisconsin–Madison. Formerly a newspaper reporter, Matt has been a science writer and research consultant for nine years. He has written more than two dozen children's books, and has written and directed a few short films. He lives in Madison with his son.